POLKO

by Angus Harrison

Polko was first performed at Paines Plough Roundabout at Summerhall
during the Edinburgh Festival Fringe in August 2023

POLKO

by Angus Harrison

Emma	**Rosie Dwyer** (she/her)
Peter	**John Macneill** (he/him)
Joe	**Elliot Norman** (he/him)
Director	**Emily Ling Williams** (she/her)
Sound Designer	**Lung Dart**
Lighting Designer	**Luca Panetta** (he/him)
Set Designer	**Evelyn Cromwell** (she/her)
Stage Manager	**Ella Godbold-Holmes** (she/her)
Producer	**RJG Productions**

With thanks to John & Helen Barnett and Paines Plough

CREDITS

Rosie Dwyer | she/her | EMMA

Rosie Dwyer is an actor from Shropshire based in London. Rosie's stage credits include: *Don't Stand So Close to Me* (Kings Head Theatre). Her TV credits include: *Fifteen Love* (Amazon Prime); *Sex Education*, *The A List* (Netflix). Her film credits include: *Death on the Nile*, directed by Kenneth Branagh. Rosie trained with the National Youth Theatre.

John Macneill | he/him | PETER

Madhainn mhath! Rugadh mi ann an Inbhir Narran, ach tha mi a' fuireach anns a' Chòrn a-nis. Bha mi a' fuireach ann am Baile Àirneach airson greis. Morning! I was born in Nairn, but I live in Cornwall now. I lived in Balerno for a while. Over the last few years, I have had some lovely jobs. I played Jacka Hoblyn in ten episodes of *Poldark*, over three series. I was in an episode each of *His Dark Materials* and *Beyond Paradise*. In theatre I was Osborne in an outdoor production of *Journey's End* at the Minack Theatre, Porthcurno, where you can watch the gannets diving into the sea while awaiting your cue. I toured as Peter in *The Coastguard*, a five-star-reviewed solo play by Marie Macneill, produced by our own company, Mundic Nation. It's great to be on stage again, and in a new play!

Elliot Norman | he/him | JOE

Elliot recently graduated from Royal Welsh College of Music and Drama. Since then he has been working in film and TV, appearing in BBC *Doctors*, the new series of *Grantchester* for ITV, and the feature film *The Great Escaper* for Pathé with Michael Caine.

Angus Harrison | he/him | Writer

Angus Harrison is a writer from Bristol. As a playwright his work has been produced for VAULT Festival and performed at the Royal Court. He was one of ten writers selected by Papatango for their *Isolated But Open* monologue collection during the pandemic, which was published by Nick Hern Books. He wrote, directed and produced a short radio play as part of the BBC's New Creatives scheme, which aired on BBC Radio 4 and was showcased at the ICA. He is currently developing multiple original ideas for television, including two script commissions, alongside writing a new play for BBC Radio 4. As a journalist he was a staff writer at *VICE* for three years, where he wrote about politics, society and nightclubs. He has also written for the *Guardian*, *Dazed*, *The Outline* and *The Face*, among others, and was nominated for a British Society of Magazine Editors award during this time.

Emily Ling Williams | she/her | Director

Emily was previously Trainee Director at Paines Plough, a Resident Director at the Almeida Theatre and Jerwood Assistant Director at the Young Vic. She is currently an Origins Artist at Headlong. As Director: *Wasted* (Lyric Hammersmith); *The Full Works*, *The Key Workers Cycle* (Almeida); *Text Me When You're Home: Five Plays* (Young Vic); *Lucky Cigarette* (New Earth); *Swallow*, *16* (Lemon House Theatre); *GYSB*, *Tuesday at the Library*, *A Perpetual State of Happiness*, *Good Trouble* (Moongate); *Appropriate*, *The Sign in Sidney Brustein's Window* (RWCMD); *Miss Julie* (LAMDA); *Preach* (Rose Bruford); *Turbines* (Paines Plough/RWCMD/Gate Theatre). As Assistant Director: *The House Of Shades* (Almeida); *Blood Wedding* (Young Vic); *The Meeting*, *The Chalk Garden* (Chichester Festival Theatre); *Black Mountain*, *Out if Love*; *How to Be a Kid* (Paines Plough/Theatr Clwyd/Orange Tree); *The Island Nation* (Arcola).

Lung Dart | Sound Designer

Tim Clay and James Rapson work together as composers and sound designers. As Lung Dart their music spans live instrumentation, sample-based productions, experimental music and pop. Alongside their Lung Dart releases they have worked with people including Turner Prize-winner Mark Leckey, Norwegian pop sensation Aurora, Hot Chip's Alexis Taylor, award-winning artist

Xnthony, and fashion designer Simone Rocha. They have scored artworks and films that have been shown at Festival de Cannes, Tate Britain, Tate Modern, Barbican Centre, BFI London Film Festival, Somerset House, Sitges Film Festival, Berlin Film Festival and many others. Recent highlights include: Score for BIFA-nominated short film *Scale* by Joseph Pierce, which premiered at Cannes 2022 as part of International Critics Week, and music production and sound design for *Oliver Cromwell is Really Very Sorry*, for which they were nominated for Best Soundscape at the Irish Theatre Awards 2023. They also have a monthly show on London's NTS Radio.

Luca Panetta | he/him | Lighting Designer

Luca works as a freelance lighting designer, video designer, and programmer. Recent Credits as Lighting & Video Designer include: *Edith* (Lowry/Theatr Clwyd); If Opera's 2022 *Season La Rondine*, *Il segreto di Susanna*, *Rita* (Belcombe Court); The Faction's 2021 *Solos* (Wilton's Music Hall); *Diary of a Somebody* (Seven Dials Playhouse), nominated for an Offie for Lighting Design; *Broken Toys* (Cervantes Theatre); The Wardrobe Ensemble's *Education, Education, Education*, *The Last of the Pelican Daughters*, directed by Sarah Frankcom (ALWF Theatre). Credits as Associate Lighting Designer include: *A Playlist for the Revolution* (Bush Theatre); *Worth* (Arcola/Storyhouse); *Cinderella* (Theatre Royal Stratford East); *The Merchant of Venice 1936* (HOME Manchester); *Cinderella: The AWESOME Truth* (Polka Theatre); *The Apology* (Arcola Theatre). Associate Video includes: *Carousel* (Susie Sainsbury Theatre); *Mind Mangler* (Mischief Theatre, UK tour and Virgin Voyages). Luca also works as a freelance lighting programmer for companies such as Hampstead Theatre, NTLive and Stratford East. Luca trained at LAMDA (London Academy of Music & Dramatic Arts) in Productional Technical Arts.

Evelyn Cromwell | she/her | Set Designer

Evelyn Cromwell as an artist living and working in Newcastle upon Tyne. Since graduating in 2017 with a degree in Glass and Ceramics, she now creates functional sculpture with a range of material. She exhibits and collaborates often, and is one half of a curatorial duo called the Spaghetti Factory, who coordinate exhibitions across the North of England.

Ella Godbold-Holmes | she/her | Stage Manager

Ella graduated from GSA with an MA in Stage and Production Management in 2021, and since then has worked on a variety of productions she is incredibly proud of. Theatre (especially fringe and independent) is made up of a lot of hard work and dedication and she is thrilled to be a part of *Polko* as the SM. Credits include: Playful Productions Workshop, Workshop Stage Manager; *Dismissed* (Soho Theatre, Stage Manager); *The Woman in Black* (West End, ASM Book Cover and ASM); *Jekyll & Hyde* schools tour (National Theatre).

RJG Productions

RJG Productions is a theatre production company focusing on new writing. The company is currently producing *It's Headed Straight Towards Us* (Park Theatre); *Polko* (Paines Plough); *Bitter Lemons* (Pleasance/Bristol Old Vic) and *Earshot* with Hot Coals Productions (UK tour). Other credits include *Brilliant Jerks* by Joseph Charlton (Southwark Playhouse); *Amélie the Musical* (Criterion Theatre, West End); award-winning *A Hundred Words for Snow* by Tatty Hennessy (Trafalgar Studios, UK tour and VAULT Festival) and the original production of *ANNA X* by Joseph Charlton. Projects in development include *Attrition* by Tatty Hennessy, a commission as part of the Writers' Guild of Great Britain New Play Scheme.

Twitter	@RJGProductions
Instagram	@rjgproductions
Facebook	@RJG Productions
Website	rjgproductions.co.uk

Press | Mobius PR

Angus Harrison

Angus Harrison is a playwright from Bristol. His work has been performed at the Royal Court and he was one of ten writers selected by Papatango for their *Isolated But Open* monologue collection during the pandemic. His radio plays *Asystole Belgravia* and *The Wire Cutters* (co-written with Joseph Charlton) were broadcast on BBC Radio 4. He is currently developing multiple original ideas for television. Prior to writing plays, Angus was a journalist, covering politics, society and nightclubs.

ANGUS HARRISON

Polko

faber

First published in 2023
by Faber and Faber Limited
The Bindery, 51 Hatton Garden
London, ECIN 8HN

Typeset by Brighton Gray
Printed and bound in the UK by CPI Group (Ltd), Croydon CR0 4YY

Angus Harrison is hereby identified as author
of this work in accordance with Section 77 of the
Copyright, Designs and Patents Act 1988

A CIP record for this book
is available from the British Library

ISBN 978-0-571-38770-0

Printed and bound in the UK on FSC® certified paper in line with our continuing
commitment to ethical business practices, sustainability and the environment.
For further information see faber.co.uk/environmental-policy

2 4 6 8 10 9 7 5 3

Acknowledgements

I would like to express enormous thanks to Emily Ling Williams, Rebecca Gwyther, Elliot Norman, Rosie Dwyer, John Macneill, Ella Godbold-Holmes, Tim Clay, James Rapson, Luca Panetta, Eve Cromwell, Katie Posner, Ellie Fitz-Gerald, Paines Plough, John Barnett and Augustine Cerf, whose faith and hard work made this play's first production possible.

I also owe a huge sum of gratitude to Elin Schofield, Jacob Sparrow, the Peggy Ramsay Foundation, Vault Festival, Joe Phillips, Flo Brockmann, Olivia Burgin, Dinah Wood, Lily Levinson, Jodi Gray, Cleo Hetherington, Deena Butt, Greg Brenman, Issy Wroe Wright, Francis Blagburn, Joe Zadeh, Perran and Emily Ellson, Claire, Mike, Dom, Mum and Dad.

The road to staging *Polko* was a long one, and the cause would have felt pretty hopeless at points were it not for the unwavering support of friends and family too numerous to mention. You know who you are. Thank you.

I will be forever indebted to my beloved Duncan and Louise, who carried and comforted me when I needed it most. And to Jenn Morgan, a champion and friend who works far too hard on my behalf.

Above all I would like to thank Joe Charlton, whose guidance and bottomless generosity unlocked all of this. And Eleanor Sutton, who first took my hand and walked me through the door.

Polko was first performed at Paines Plough Roundabout at Summerhall during the Edinburgh Festival Fringe in August 2023. The cast, in alphabetical order, was as follows:

Emma Rosie Dwyer
Peter John Macneill
Joe Elliot Norman

Director Emily Ling Williams
Sound Designer Lung Dart
Lighting Designer Luca Panetta
Set Designer Evelyn Cromwell
Stage Manager Ella Godbold-Holmes
Producer RJG Productions

Characters

Joe
late twenties

Emma
late twenties

Peter
fifties

Setting

This play is set in the outskirts of a city in South-West England. An urban fringe: not quite a town, but not quite a village. Not somewhere especially bad, but not somewhere especially good. All the action takes place in the front seats of a parked car. Characters should mostly face forward. Eye contact should be sparing. Light costume changes should take place between scenes where possible, to indicate the passing of time.

This play is, among other things, about boredom. Boredom should live inside it. It should feel like nothing is going to happen, so intensely that the world could crack open any minute through the sheer force of the listlessness. Set should be minimal and lighting tightly framed. The short wordless scenes should be punchy, like strobes hitting stained-glass windows.

POLKO

'In any case life is but a procession of shadows, and God knows why it is that we embrace them so eagerly, and see them depart with such anguish, being shadows.'

Virginia Woolf, *Jacob's Room*

'Real life, just around the corner . . .'

Prefab Sprout

Notes

– indicates an interruption.

/ means the next character should begin speaking.

, on its own line indicates a pause of a few seconds
or longer.

A space between lines indicates a more momentary beat.

ONE

*Two car seats. Grey patterned fabric, loose seatbelts. Before
the play begins: music, but muffled, as if coming from inside
the car.*
Lights dim to black.
*Lights up, sharp. A small pool that coats the car seats in low,
yellow light. The radio is on; LOUD. Something soulful,
from the 1970s. Magic FM or Smooth.*
*Peter sits in the driver's seat. He's drunk and agitated. He
listens to the radio and drinks from a bottle of white wine
that he keeps in a blue plastic bag on the passenger seat.*
*He wipes his mouth and puts the bottle back in the bag. He
rummages around in the bag again, removes a charging cable
for a phone and dumps it on the passenger seat. Next he
removes a small black box from his jacket pocket, looks at it,
then puts it back.*
*He gathers himself, wraps the handles of the blue bag tightly
around his wrist, then reaches up to press the interior
reading light above him.*
Blackout.

*

Darkness.

Joe	Alright?

Emma Yeh alright.
Can you hold that?

Joe Yeh.
No probs give it here I'll.
Cheers.

Emma Sorry got all my
stuff everywhere.

There's always one too many things for one bag.
Then you end up starting a new bag. /
Now I've got all this shite.

Joe   You shouldn't put your uh
toothbrush in the same bag as your books.

Emma   Oh bollocks.
Yeh.
That was a last-minute decision.

Joe   Are you nervous?

Emma   No.
Not nervous no.
How come?

Joe flicks a lighter and the car interior is illuminated.
He lets go but the light remains.
Joe and Emma are revealed. They sit next to each
other, Joe in the driver's seat, Emma on the passenger
side, a duffel bag at her feet and a hot-water bottle
clutched to her stomach. Joe is holding a carrier bag
containing some of her other possessions. They both
look up through the windscreen to the lit windows of
a house, somewhere above them.

Joe   You're giving off a uh
very distinct mood.
Just trying to find the right word for it.

Emma   Ha right.
Okay yeh sorta.
Not nervous just . . .

Joe   Waiting like . . .
Expectant?

Emma   Yeh.
Expectant. /
Right.

Joe   Or.
        Is there a word for like
        the feeling of waiting?
        You know.
        Just before something.

Emma   I don't.
        Antici-
        patory?
        No not. /
        I don't know.

Joe   Yeh maybe but like.
        There must be a word for the feeling of waiting.

Emma   I –
        (*Shrugs.*)
        I don't know.
        I'm sorry.
        Thanks let me.
        (*Takes the carrier bag.*)
        I'll take that back.
        (*To herself.*) Okay.
        Okay.
        (*To Joe.*) Thanks for the lift
        by the way.

Joe   Eh no bother.

Emma   Okay.

Joe   When are they expecting you?

Emma   Hm?

Joe   Do they know you're back?

Emma   They know I'm back tonight yeh.
        Didn't give them a specific time just . . .

Joe   Right.

| Emma | Fancy driving us around the block? |
| | Or . . . |

| Joe | Ha. / |
| | Well if you want . . . |

| Emma | (*to herself*) Okay. |
| | (*To Joe.*) No it's okay. |

| Joe | They'll be pleased to see you. |
| | Won't they? |

Emma	Eh.
	Who can tell.
	Is anyone pleased to see anyone
	do you know what I mean?

| Joe | Well. |
| | I'm pleased to see you. |

| Emma | (*smiles*) Ah |
| | thank you. |

They pretend 'cheers' two invisible cups. This relaxes Emma somehow. She falls back into her seat.

D'you wanna come in?

| Joe | Um. |

| Emma | Just to say hello. / |
| | You don't have to. |

Joe	Yeh.
	Nah.
	It's okay.
	I said I'd get back.
	Mum's cooked so.

| Emma | Course. |

Joe	Get used to that by the way.
	Meal times.
	Now you're living at home I mean.
	Are you ready to have meal times again?

Emma I hadn't even thought about it.

Joe Well.
Better start.

Emma I should come and see your mum at some point.

Joe Oh yeh yeh.
She'd love that.
Any time.

Emma How's she doing she alright?

Joe Oh yeh
fine.

Emma And your sister?

Joe Yeh well.
She visits you know.

Emma She still at the water company?

Joe Yep yeh.

Emma In uh . . .

Joe Swindon.

Emma Swindon yeh.

,

(*Grinning.*) What about um.
Your mum's friend.
He still around?
Peter.

Joe Oh yeh.
The big man.
Well he's been up to all sorts.

Emma Yeh?

Joe Oh yeh.

Emma Come on gimme.

17

Joe   Um.
        Well number one.
        You're in his car.
        Well my car now
        but
        used to be his car.

Emma   Oh what?
        I thought you bought this?

Joe   I did.
        Off him.
        He sold it to me cheap as a bit of favour.
        On the condition that I give him lifts
        as and when he needs 'em.
        So I take him to play pool on Thursdays.
        Work a couple of times a week.

Emma   Why?

Joe   Uhm.
        He was broke I guess.
        Plus he got done for drink driving so.

Emma   Oh man.

Joe   Yeh.

Emma   Did something
        bad
        happen
        or?

Joe   No not really.
        He got picked up
        driving eighty down some
        country lane.
        Plastered.
        You know.
        So.

Emma God
Peter.
What a fucken weirdo.

Joe Yep.
I know.
And uh.

Emma What?

Joe He sorta –
Hah.
Sorta asked my mum to marry him.

Emma NO.

Joe Yeh.

Emma WHEN?

Joe Um.
This was about three months ago.
Three four months ago.
Same night he lost his licence actually.
Halloween I think. /
Yeh Halloween.

Emma Hold on
go back.
Same night as the driving?

Joe Yeh.

Emma Wait just.
Start again and tell me everything.

Joe Hah.
Um.
So.
We're in the pub.
In the uh
Stag.

About eight.
And we're all sitting there,
it's karaoke night and we're all watching some guy singing
I don't know what
and it's just me and Mum
and Cathy from her work.
Few quiet ones you know.
And then Peter bundles in.
And you know when –
You know when someone uh
brings their outside energy in?
And they can't shake it off.
He's like that.
Brings the wind in around his shoulders.
Falls through the room.
Can't settle in his seat.
Up to the bar and back every five minutes.
Getting rounds in for everyone.
Which he can't afford.
Uhm.
And we're all saying like
Pete mate just grab a seat you know?
Have a scotch!
Settle down!
But he's antsy.
So anyway
we leave him to it.
Next thing we know
he's put his name down on the clipboard
to sing that Smokey Robinson song.
You know /
'Being with You'.

Emma Yeh yeh yeh.

Joe So he gets up
and it's

emotional like.
Pretty raw.
He's living it
properly living it
every word. /
And uh . . .

Emma No no no.

Joe Yeh so he gets to the end of that and –
Oh he's got like a
bag
by the way
the whole time
a blue plastic bag hanging around his wrist.

Emma Right.

Joe So he finishes his song.
Polite applause.
And he yanks the bag off
fishes around in it for what feels like forever and then
pulls out a fucken
really expensive old ring.
No cheapskate shite.
Like a proper antique
rock.

Emma No Peter.

Joe Uh-huh.
And yeh
gets down on one knee
and speaks into the mic
says
Debbie girl –

Emma Girl!

Joe Yep
Debbie girl

I should have told you this before
but we're meant to be.
We're meant to be.
All that sort of stuff.
I can't really remember.

Emma   And what did your mum say?

Joe   Well she was obviously.
I mean they've never even.
They've been pals for fucken years!
And even when her and Dad split you know
He never seemed interested in *that* way.
So she was pretty
floored.

Emma   Did she say no though?

Joe   Oh yeh.
Did it nice and all.
But yeh she said no.
She was pretty angry.
Hasn't spoken to him since.
Silent treatment
you know.

Emma   Christ.
Pete.
Wasn't everyone watching?
What did she actually say?

Joe   I believe she said
It's getting late Peter.
Come and have a sit-down.

Emma   Wow.

Joe   Yeh.

Emma   You're living in a soap opera.

Joe   Yeh right.
Well . . .

Emma Oh and what about Polko?
I meant to text him but I don't have his current number
I don't think.

Joe Yeh that's . . .

Emma What?

Joe That's a whole thing.
His family went sorta crazy last year.
I don't exactly know what happened but nobody can get hold of him.

Emma Shit.
Right
cos I saw on Facebook something about him moving.
But then he's deleted all his accounts and whatever.

Joe Yeh he's like
completely un-
contactable.

Emma Tara seemed to think he'd joined the navy /
or something.

Joe The navy?

Emma Yeh. /
Well that's what she thought.

Joe Nah he hasn't joined the navy.
At least I don't think he has.
(*To himself.*) The navy . . .
Can you imagine?
Polko joining the navy.
Sorry the idea of that –

Emma Yeh well.

Joe I don't think he can swim.

Emma Well do you know where he is?

Joe	I don't
	no
	is the truth.

| Emma | At all? |

| Joe | Nope. |

| Emma | That's crazy. |

| Joe | Well |
| | we hadn't actually been hanging out that much lately. |

| Emma | Oh. |
| | When did you last see him? |

Joe	Um.
	That is a good question.
	I'm going to say . . .
	Not Christmas.

| Emma | *Christmas!* |

| Joe | No *not* Christmas. |
| | Fuck's sake! |

| Emma | That's like a month ago. |

| Joe | *Not* Christmas. |

| Emma | Okay. |
| | So 'Not Christmas'. |

Joe	Yep.
	Not Christmas.
	Hah.
	Sorry
	I'm just trying to
	cast my mind back.

| Emma | That's okay. |

| Joe | Uhm. |
| | Okay I think. |

I think I saw him around Bonfire Night.
Because.
Yep
definitely Bonfire Night.
Because I remember
fireworks.

Emma That's even worse Joe.
That's ages.

Joe Well yeh.
It is sort of.
But to be honest.
He's always been a pretty flaky guy you know.
Flight of fancy probably took him off somewhere.

Emma Hm maybe.
But three months –

Joe It's difficult.
You know.
To speak about.

,

(*Looking up at window.*)
The lights are still on.
You gotta go in at some point.

Emma Hm?
Oh.
I know.
I'm just.
Enjoying this.

Joe What have you told them?

Emma Not all of it.
Obviously that I lost my job.
Redundancy and all that.
None of the rest of it.

Which is worse in a way I suppose.
Because I'll get it in the neck
about the job
with no context.
No awareness of all the other stuff.

Joe What other stuff?

Emma (*sighs.*)
Let's do that another time.
(*Semi-sarcastic.*) I'm a very sick woman Joe.

*Emma puts her hot-water bottle into the carrier bag
and prepares herself to go inside. Then pauses.*

,

I've wasted so much time.
That's how it feels.
So much time.

Joe Well no.
Don't say that.
I'm sure there'll be lots you'll take
you know
from the experience and what have you.
Life lessons.
And so on.

Emma You think do you?

Joe Not really.

Emma No.

,

Joe Listen to this.

*Joe turns on the car radio. It makes a very strange
sound. Voices and music trying to fight through a fog
of static and echo; radar blips and choirs; the song of
the ether. Joe and Emma listen for a few seconds.*

Emma What the fuck.

Joe	(*turns it off*) I know.

Emma   Do you not just need to tune it?

Joe   Nope.
Whatever you do it just makes that noise.
Thing's fully bust.

Emma   That's horrible.

Joe   I quite like it.
I've taken to putting it on and driving around.

Emma   What an image.

,

God this is weird.
Don't you find this weird?
Us being here together . . .

Joe   Not really.

Emma   Do you not?
It's like.
Like time's stuck or something.
Like we're still at school or something.
I mean I've been back obviously
to visit and whatever.
But like.
Knowing I'm back here for good is –

Joe   Back from the big city eh.

Emma   No like!
You know to be back here
moving in with my parents.
My childhood bedroom.
I don't know.
It feels like I'm on drugs or something.
Like I'm under anaesthetic.
Do you know what I mean?

Joe   Well I have been here for good.

Emma   Yeh.
            Course. /
            Sorry.
            Yeh.

Joe   And I do live with my mum.
            So.

Emma   Sorry.

            ,

Joe   Nah I do sort of know what you mean.
            The drugs thing.
            It's like.
            I sometimes think I can hear this talking.
            And I think . . .
            What if maybe
            I'm in a coma
            and that's the sound of somebody trying to wake
            me up.
            You know?

Emma   Right.

Joe   Similar,
            maybe.

            It'll be alright.
            You'll settle in.
            And you know
            it's like –
            It's never as bad as it seems.

            Emma squeezes Joe's hand. He looks down.

Emma   Thanks mate. /
            Really that's . . .

Joe   Ah no problem.
            No problem at all.

            They both return their gaze to the window up above.
            Blackout.

TWO

Lights up.
Joe sits in the driver's seat, Peter on the passenger side. He's
sober now. He holds his keys in his hands and plays with
them nervously.

Peter   They did a survey
of the whole area.
and it turns out most people live in areas at risk of –
Or at least the possibility of –
flash flooding
or flooding of some kind.
Something like seventy, eighty per cent.
It's deeply concerning really.

           ,

How are you finding her?

Joe   Yeh fine.
Good.

Peter   Yeh she's a lovely car.
I always enjoyed driving her.
My friend Dick Parsons
told me I needed to get the clutch plate looked at.
Any problems with the box
in that regard?

Joe   Nah.
No.

Peter   Right.

Joe   You can pop in if you want.

Peter   No.
No I'd better get back.
But your mum's . . . ?

Joe   Yeh she's fine.

Peter	Good.
	Good.
	And you're . . . ?

Joe	Yeh all good.

Peter	Has your mum said anything –

Joe	Obviously it's just difficult cos like.
	I can't speak for her.
	And she's still pretty angry – /
	You know?

Peter	No no.
	Of course not.

Joe	So.

,

But like if you want to try and say hello. /
It's no problem.

Peter	Nope.
	No that's fine.
	I'll be on my way.

Blackout.

THREE

Lights up.
Joe and Emma are eating a takeaway in the car.

Joe	It's all completely made up.
	That's the big secret.
	You turn up and they tell you like
	these are our company values and it's like:
	What the fuck are you talking about?
	You're a hotel.
	How can you have values?

Like
a hotel doesn't have a moral code. /
It doesn't –

Emma   This is it.
And people would always say to me:
You should take more pride in your work.

Joe   Right.

Emma   But like
how much pride can I take in this job?
I'm creating B2B marketing materials.
Do you know what that means?

Joe   Uh.
What,
do I?
No.

Emma   No.
Exactly.
Because it doesn't mean anything.
Business-to-business marketing.
I was working for a company,
who wrote emails,
on behalf of another company,
which nobody then read.
Do you know what that does to your
state of mind?

Joe   Yeh that sounds.
Really boring.

Emma   And they come out with all this
crap
about your value.
Like
how much you mean to them
blah-di-blah.
And then what happens?

You get sick
and they fire you.

Joe Wait
They fired you cos you got –
Cos of the pain thing?

Emma Not exactly.

,

My boss decided
for genuinely like
no reason
that he didn't like me.

Joe What do you mean?

Emma He just didn't like me.
I don't know what else to say.
I don't know what I did.
Whether I was bad at my job
or
wronged him in some way
but the guy just
fundamentally
didn't like me.
And.
I couldn't get my head around it.
Why won't you talk to me?
I honestly nearly emailed him asking.
I had it sitting there in my drafts like:
Why?
I demand to know.
You know?

Joe He wouldn't talk to you?

Emma Totally ignored me.
And then would like
dig me out in front of the whole team
during a meeting

just saying
Emma have you done this yet?
Something he knew I hadn't done.
And like
he'd withhold information from me.
Information I needed to do my job.
Also he took our entire team out for dinner at this
really nice bao restaurant.
You know what bao are right?
Bao buns.

Joe   Yeh.

Emma   He took everyone out and didn't invite me.
Just didn't –

Sorry.
I know it doesn't sound like a big deal but it.
It builds up.

Joe   No it's.
I mean you should have told someone.

Emma   Well I did in the end.
I emailed all the management people and HR and
I told them I wanted to quit.
That's what started the whole thing.

Joe   And what did they say?

Emma   They um –
They ignored it.
Then the following week we had an all-office meeting.
They got everyone together and said
we're having to make cutbacks,
there will be some redundancies . . .
And I was gone by lunchtime.

,

You know I wonder if maybe we're on the edge of a
massive revolution.

Everyone I know is quitting their jobs and like –
Or losing them!
What if just
nobody went back?

Joe   Yeh.
        Maybe.
        Cos also like.
        This is the thing.
        People like to think that their job gives them all this
        status and blah blah blah.
        I'm just like.
        Okay so I work in a hotel
        but I actually like that?
        Because it doesn't drag me into all this other crap.
        I know exactly how much I'm going to earn.
        And I budget for exactly what I need to spend.

Emma   You don't have to buy food though
        right?
        Cos you live with your mum.

Joe   Actually I have to buy and cook one meal a week.
        Sort of a house rule.

Emma   Okay.

Joe   But like.
        Going back to the work thing.
        It's like.
        Yes.
        I work in a hotel.
        Room service, reception
        sometimes the restaurant whatever.
        But I get paid,
        I go home,
        and I chill the fuck out.
        It leaves my brain.
        Not everything has to be some
        journey in the depths of your soul.

You can just have a job and then chill.
I think anyway.
Do you know what I mean?

Emma   Sure.
       I know what you mean.

Joe   Also there are something like
       Five –
       Six hundred locations in the country.
       So if I wanted to move to another part of the UK
       I'm basically guaranteed a job.
       Which is a perk.

Emma   But like
       surely it's not what you want to do forever.

Joe   Uh.
       I sort of don't really think in terms of forever.
       Things are like
       pretty fucked globally
       and stuff.

Emma   Right.
       But you must get bored?

Joe   Um.
       Not really.
       You get to see some pretty cool stuff.

       I'm pretty sure some people shot a porn film there a
       couple of months ago
       for example.
       In one of the rooms.

Emma   WHAT!
       How did you know?

Joe   Uh.
       A suspiciously large group of people checked into a
       double room.
       In the middle of the afternoon.

And the guy who had the booking was like
a perv.
He just had a very
sexual look to him.
Then housekeeping said the floor was all
covered in bin bags.

Emma   That's disgusting.

Joe   Hah.
I know.

*Emma's gaze returns to the window; lost in
thought.*

Emma   I think I'm going to stay here for a while.
Living I mean.
I feel good.
I think it's good for me.
It's cleansing me.

Joe   Great.

Emma   You're pleased about that?

Joe   I'm –
Yeh I think that's wicked.
With your parents or will you try and find
somewhere or . . .

Emma   With my parents for now I think.

Joe   That's cool.
People generally turn their noses up at like
living with a parent
or parents or whatever
and actually
it's pretty sweet.
Like
my mum works so much anyway she's hardly ever
there.
I basically have my own place.

Emma   Maybe I'll find somewhere eventually.
        I just feel incredibly still
        at the moment.
        I'm doing a lot of reflecting on things that have
        happened
        and just sort of
        processing my life and what's led me to this point and
        I think I've been trying to keep myself busy
        basically
        to distract me from something.
        And I don't know what that something is.
        It's something deep down in me.
        But I've been drowning it out you know.
        Like trying to ignore it.

Joe   Yeh.

Emma   Do you know what I mean?

Joe   Yeh totally.

Emma   Yesterday I just sat on the sofa for an hour.
        Just this big sofa my parents have
        and I didn't do anything.
        I didn't look at my phone.
        I didn't turn on the TV.
        I just sank down into myself and –
        It was so
        lush and deep.
        I don't know . . .

Joe   My mum is pretty insistent on me not using the sofa
        at ours.
        Which is pretty annoying.

Emma   Right.

Joe   She says it's hers.
        It's this weird fabric
        and I got some oil on it.

Emma   Oil?

Joe Yeh like.
       Chilli oil.

Emma Oh.

Joe Which is:
       Okay I get it that that's annoying
       but you don't have to banish me to another chair.
       I'm not a dog.

Emma Right yeh.

Joe It's all territorial shit.
       That's why the car is good.
       It's like private space.
       Like if I get in late
       after a big night or whatever
       and I know she's got an early start
       and she's gonna get pissy with me you know
       I can just sleep it off in the car and wait until she's
       gone to work.

Emma You sleep in the car?

Joe No!
       Only if I've had a big night –
       Been getting on it –
       Anyway.
       Not that I do that anymore.
       It's just a back-up.
       And cos you said about
       personal space or whatever.

       ,

       Do you remember Kai Martin?

Emma Who?

Joe Kai Martin.
       He broke into our school once and slept there.

Emma Oh right.
       Maybe.

Joe   He just moved back as well.
        Lives with his parents.

Emma   Oh okay.
        Have you seen him?

Joe   No.
        I don't really know him.
        Just know that he's back.

Emma   If you don't mind me asking.
        Who do you
        hang out with now?

Joe   What do you mean?

Emma   Well if Polko's not around
        who are like –
        Who do you see?

Joe   You?

Emma   Well yeh but besides me.
        Before I got here.

Joe   Oh.
        I have friends.

Emma   Yeh?

Joe   Yeh.
        Some guys who work at the hotel.
        Some guys who uh.
        Do you remember Sarah Tanner?

Emma   Yeh right.
        I think.

Joe   I see her in the Stag all the time.

Emma   Right.

Joe   So yeh.
        Loads of people.
        Plus.

I don't know about you but.
I'm increasingly in favour of being alone.
Not all the time but.
I basically have zero obligations to the outside world.
I'm very independent in that sense.
It's a strength.

Emma   Well sure
       you've got to be happy by yourself.

Joe   Exactly.

Emma   But that doesn't mean you should
       want to be by yourself.

Joe   I'm not by myself.
       I already told you.
       Fucken
       Sarah Tanner.

Emma   Okay!

       ,

       You know.
       When I lost my job.
       That was really difficult because I didn't really have
       anyone to talk to about it.
       I had friends.
       Or people I thought were friends.
       But they were more like
       people who moved around
       inside my life.
       They weren't a part of my life itself
       do you see what I mean?

Joe   Uh sort of yeh.

       ,

Emma   Did I tell you about the night the pain started?

Joe   Not that I recall.

Emma Hm.

I woke up in the middle of the night
And had this feeling
right here in the top of my belly that was like –
Like I'd eaten a load of smashed glass.

Joe Ouch.

Emma It was around the time I got the sack.
I was writhing around in bed
and I grabbed my phone
and I distinctly remember having this moment where
I was like:
Well holy shit.
I have nobody to call.
I don't have a person to call in this situation.
And that was uh.
That was a bad feeling.
Really bad.

Joe You could have uh
called me if you wanted.

Emma Bless you but.
I mean it's great we're seeing each other now but.
It's been a while you know?

Joe I know but like.
We're old pals man.
You can always.

Emma Yeh but we're not like –

Joe What?

Emma Nothing it's fine.
That's nice.

,

Joe So what was it?
The pain . . .

Emma   I still don't know.
Every doctor I saw just tried to tell me it was my
period.
Or that I was stressed.
Remains unexplained.

Joe   You know I read about these
families of lumberjacks in America.
This was in the 1800s or something.
Who had an unexplained medical condition
that made them jump into the air.
Like they'd just go rigid and
shoot up into the air.
Like they were being fired out of cannons.

Emma   Wow.
Did they find out what caused it?

Joe   Uhhh.
I'm not sure.
It might have been uh . . .
What's the . . .
Hereditary.

,

Emma   Does my breath smell?

Joe   Breathe on me.

Emma   What just . . .

Joe   Yeh.

She breathes in his face.

No.
A bit.
Not bad just smells like
a mouth
you know.

Does it hurt right now?

42

Emma   Hm?

Joe   Your stomach?

Emma   A bit.
Sort of backgroundy.

Joe   I wish I could make it better.

Emma   (*laughing*) Joe.
What do you mean?

Joe   (*playing along*) Like
find a cure or something.
Maybe I could do some research.

Emma   Well I have to go to the doctors again.
Next week.
For a scan.
It's kinda important and.
You could take me maybe?
I don't want to tell my mum and my dad –
I can't be doing
all of that
you know.
I love him but.
My dad worries enough about me being like
unemployed
and vitamin-D deficient.
Last thing I need is him asking me about my
phantom whatever
you know?

Joe   Yeh fine.
I mean.
Depends what time.
But yeh.
Fine.

Blackout.

FOUR

Lights up gradually.
Joe sits alone in the car, looking at his phone. The screen is
absurdly bright and should light his face from beneath. The
car radio plays a podcast about something very obscure:
quantum computing or something similar.
Slow fade to blackout.

*

Lights up sharp.
Peter is in the passenger seat again. They sit in silence. Joe has
the car's hazard lights switched on. A rhythmic ticking and
the blink of an orange light.

,

Peter   I still remember farthings.
            If you can believe that.
            I mean.
            We're talking here about
            a coin the size of a robin's egg.

            ,

            I got you something.

Joe   Oh.

Peter   It's whisky.

Joe   Oh right.

Peter   Uhp.

Joe   What's this for.

Peter   Oh you know.
            Driving me to and fro.
            And also just –
            Well there we are.

It's an Islay malt.
Do you know what that means?

Joe   No.

Peter   Islay is where it's made.
        It's a Hebridean island.
        So this is an Islay malt.
        I don't like 'em.

Joe   Okay.

Peter   Try a bit.

Joe   What just?

Peter   Yeh have a sip.
        Go on.

Joe   I gotta drive.

Peter   One little sip won't –
        Go on.
        Get it down you lad.

Joe   Okay.

Peter   (*mutters*) Get it down you.
        There we go.

Joe   Uh-huh.

Peter   Yep.
        I mean.
        As I say.
        I don't like them.
        Islays.
        But.
        Yeh.
        Makes everything feel numb doesn't it?

Joe   I guess yeh.
        Thanks.

Peter   Oh that's no problem.

Joe   Um.
        You said you had
        something to show me?

Peter   Oh yup.
        Hold on.

        Peter retrieves a plastic wallet full of paper from the carrier bag at his feet. He starts removing sheets he's printed out.

        I might have mentioned this to you before at some point.
        But I've been getting quite into family history.
        Researching it online and working out
        family trees and –
        You can go quite far back.
        It's quite impressive really.

Joe   Okay.

Peter   So if you look here.
        This is a map.
        A pretty good map of your family tree
        going back to 1788.

Joe   Okay.

Peter   So you know . . .
        I can talk you through it
        if you want some details?

Joe   Uh sure.
        That sounds interesting.

Peter   I just think it's good for a person to know their family history.
        It's good to have a sense of
        the who the what and the why
        of

	you if you see what I mean.
Joe	Wait hold on. Is this your family. Or. Is this my family tree?
Peter	Yeh this is . . .
Joe	You've done my family history?
Peter	Yeh.
Joe	Like you've – Did you pay for this?
Peter	A bit yeh.
Joe	And you didn't do yours? You did mine.
Peter	Yeh. You and your mum's yeh.
Joe	That's – Okay.
Peter	I just thought it would be good for you to know about.
Joe	Okay. It's actually –
Peter	What?
Joe	That feels quite invasive.
Peter	What does?
Joe	This.
Peter	(*taking the paper back*) Oh I get everything wrong.

| Joe | Like you should ask / |
| | before you . . . |

Peter	It's not.
	I haven't hacked your bank account.
	I've compiled some information.

| Joe | It's just. |
| | Hm. |

| Peter | It's publicly available. |
| | It's all out there. |

| Joe | Yeh but like. |
| | It's weird to not ask before doing something like this. |

Peter	Sorry.
	I didn't want to upset you.
	I was trying to be nice.
	It's a gesture.
	I get everything wrong.

,

| Joe | What uh. |
| | What did you find. |

| Peter | There's lots of really cool stuff in here. |

| Joe | Yeh? |

Peter	Absolutely.
	Your family was in the newspaper here.
	Your great-great-uncle.
	A man called Ernest.
	Arrived home to find his wife and baby
	dead in a peggy tub.

Joe	Shit.
	What uh.
	What's a peggy tub?

| Peter | (*returns to the text*) A peggy tub . . . |
| | Is . . . |

A type of bathtub I'd assume.
But I'd have to check that.

Joe   How did they die?

Peter   They were.
Suicide.
Well.
Suicide murder.

Joe   Oh.

Peter   Ernest was a drinker.
Who spent all of his wages on –
Here's a court transcript –
On booze.

Joe   Right.
Shit.

Peter   You can read there . . .
(*Reading from the print-out.*) *The Deputy Coroner:*
Did you often want a drink?
That depends.
Twice a day?
Yes.
Haven't Mr and Mrs Bancroft, your neighbours,
cautioned you about your wife's condition?
They have said she felt lonely.
So on so on . . .
And then . . .
Witness in reply to other questions admitted that he
took his wife's watch to repair
and pawned it unknown to her.
He spent the money on food and some was expended
in drink.
He denied that he had got into trouble with the
police.

You were away from home on Tuesday evening from
six until ten o'clock.

49

How many public houses did you go into in that time?
Four.
Drinks in each of course?
I had naturally a drink in each.
Weren't you very anxious to get back to your wife?
Yes, it was raining and I was wet through.
And it goes on like that for a while.
I did bring
a folder
plastic wallet thing
for you to put all this in.

Joe   Okay great.
        Thanks.
        That's great.

Peter   So you'll show your mum that?

Joe   Uh yeh.
        I guess.

Peter   She loves her history.
        I think she'll find it really interesting.

Joe   I guess.
        Right.
        Thanks.

        Blackout.

FIVE

Music. LOUD breakbeats filtered through the radio's foggy hiss.
Lights up sharp.
Emma is dressed up for a night out that has just ended. Joe has stayed up to pick her up and take her home. She is drunk and trying to be sick into a carrier bag.
She hands Joe her phone.

Emma   CAN YOU HOLD THIS.

Joe   Yep.

Emma   I DON'T ACTUALLY THINK.
(*Retches.*)
No.
I DON'T ACTUALLY THINK I'M GOING TO BE
SICK.
IT JUST TASTES LIKE IT.
ACID.
YOU KNOW?
UGH.

Joe   You okay?

Emma   Yeh.

Joe   Worth it?

Emma   CAN YOU TURN THAT OFF?

Joe   Sorry.

*Joe hits the radio. Emma shuts her eyes and hangs
her head as the urge to vomit gradually subsides.*

Emma   Thank you.
What did you say?

Joe   How was the night?

Emma   Fine.
I guess.
I just felt old.
Everyone was so young.

Joe   I thought you were with Katie . . .

Emma   Oh I was.
I just mean.
In the actual club
everyone was young.

Joe	Oh. I'm not surprised. I haven't been in there in like a decade.
Emma	You don't realise you're old until you're face to face with it.
Joe	At least eight years.
Emma	Until you see an eighteen-year-old up close you know.
Joe	I'm actually surprised it's still open.
Emma	They have these round soft marzipan faces. Do you know what I mean?
Joe	Uh. Marzipan . . . No?
Emma	And they don't even drink.
Joe	Yeh.
Emma	Like half of them. Most of them don't even drink. *What the fuck are you doing here?*
Joe	That's a bit of a misconception actually.
Emma	What is?
Joe	That people don't drink anymore.
Emma	Right.
Joe	People are actually drinking much much more than at any time in human history.

I read.
Globally. /
Mainly in low-income countries actually.

Emma Katie is also.
She has grown into a very boring person in the last
ten years.
Very
two-dimensional.
She's realised she wants to be a yoga teacher.
Or is training to become –
I was like.
Come on.
That's your big discovery about yourself?
Everyone's a fucken yoga teacher.
Get a real job.
You know what I mean?

Joe I guess.

Emma And she didn't ask me anything about myself.
Don't you hate that?
When someone just keeps going about themselves.
Non-stop.

Joe I thought she worked on a boat.

Emma I don't understand how some people have such
a a a
bad grasp on how to hold a conversation.
It's not that hard.

Joe A yacht or a cruise or something . . .

Emma You talk for a bit and then someone talks back.

Joe Totally.

Emma People are just –
Some people are so
self-centred.
Ask me a question!!!

Joe   What *me?*

Emma   No.
        I'm saying Katie didn't.
        (*Laughing.*) No you're fine.

Joe   Well maybe she's not the friend you thought she was.
        There's a lot of people think you should just
        get rid of friends you don't need.

Emma   Yes.
        Thank you.
        Exactly.

        *Emma feels queasy again so returns to some heavy
        breathing. She briefly shuts her eyes. Reopens them.
        She's antsy drunk. The alcohol is making her restless
        and itchy; she tunes into buried feelings and then
        turns away from them.*

        Do you ever drink drive?
        Be honest.

Joe   No.
        No sir.
        I sometimes have 'a beer' but that's fine.
        You're allowed to do that.

Emma   Okay.
        Don't drink drive.
        Promise?

Joe   Yup.
        I promise.

Emma   I like this car.
        It's sort of horrible but I like it.
        It's a good place for something bad like a
        breakdown or –

Joe   Are you
        planning
        on having a breakdown?

Emma   Am I?
          Uh hah.
          Yes.
          No.
          I am.
          I'm tired of thinking.
          I think one day I'm going to think so hard about
          something
          that my brain just
          supernovas
          and explodes inside my skull.
          Do you have that?

Joe   Uhm.
          Naaat really no.

Emma   So you're always
          just
          so relaxed?

Joe   I'm not always relaxed.
          I just don't let shit get over the top you know.
          People love drama.

Emma   I love drama?

Joe   No not you.
          Just everyone like thinks they've got something
          wrong with them.
          I'm just like.
          It's fine.
          I'm fine you know.

Emma   Right.
          Do you think I'm
          worrying more than I should be then?

Joe   No I'm not saying that I'm just . . .

Emma   But you do think I'm overreact–
          I overreact
          to stuff.

Joe   No I just think like.
        Some people want to be complicated.
        Not saying you do.

Emma   But people are complicated.
        Aren't they?

Joe   (*shrugs*) Depends.

Emma   On what?

Joe   It has to do with like
        how . . .

Emma   Mhm . . .

Joe   . . . you measure
        your life.
        I just think it's very easy to end up in a place where
        you're always expecting more.
        And asking yourself
        why don't I have that?
        What's wrong with me?
        And I think that drives people crazy.

Emma   So you don't want anything?

Joe   No I do.
        I just make sure that I want things I can definitely
        get.

Emma   I'm gonna sleep in your car.

Joe   Okay then . . .

        Emma turns onto her side and closes her eyes. After a
        few seconds she opens them again and looks up at
        Joe.

Emma   I always remember you and Polko made those
        comedy sketch
        videos.
        They were funny.

Joe   Yeh.
       I actually had to contact YouTube about getting
       those taken down.

Emma   Oh.
       You were both very sweet boys.
       I liked being around you both because
       you loved each other so much.

Joe   Well that's.
       Nice.

Emma   I think it's sad you had an argument or whatever.

Joe   Yeh well.
       He just got very difficult to be around.

Emma   In what way?

Joe   He just had some
       troubled dealings.

Emma   What does that mean?

Joe   He was troubled.

Emma   Tell me about it.

Joe   Tell you about what?

Emma   What was troubling him.

Joe   Uhm.
       Hah.
       Uhhhh.
       He was in a bad way for a while.
       Like
       depressed and off the rails and stuff.
       Kind of torpedoing himself into the ground really.
       He lost his job at the start of last year.
       Same as you really.
       A 'we don't need you' type thing.
       So

he was done with that.
And there's nothing else you know.
What are you going to do?
He tried getting other stuff for a bit.
But that was gone too.
And he didn't have good people around him.

Emma   How do you mean?

Joe   He fell in with a sort of bad crowd
I guess you'd say.
Bad influences.
And he was bored.
He was so fucken bored and.
It was just a great big nothing for so,
so,
long.
And then
he had a uh . . .
Experience?
I guess you'd call it.

Emma   What experience?

Joe   It's weird mind.
Hah.
Don't –
A like
mystical thing happened to him
at a party.

Emma   What do you mean.

Joe   In
September.
I met these guys at work.
They were staying at the hotel.
In town for a conference.
I got chatting to them at reception and
they seemed pretty sound you know?
Decent enough guys.

I clocked off and picked up Polko.
Like I always did you know.
We'd drive around and grab some drinks whatever.

Emma   Right.
Sure.

Joe   But these guys they'd said they were going to have
some drinks in their room.
Smoke some hash so whatever.
We went up.
And.
It was a long night.
I don't remember all of it.
Anyhow
I went off with this guy to get more booze and we
lost track of time.
And when I got back to the hotel
the room was trashed.
So I'm already thinking like
man I'm going to get fired now.
And I can't find Polko.
And I'm asking them like:
Have you seen my friend?
Have you seen Polko?
you know
and none of them is answering.
One of them is passed out completely.
It's a bit of war zone to be honest.
And then finally one of them says:
The roof.
You've got to go to the roof.
So I'm like
well shit
that's bad news whichever way you look at it right?
The fucken roof.
So I go charging out the room.
Through the fire exit.

Anyway he wasn't quite up there.
He was sat on his own on this little stair –
Landing – /
Type –

Emma   Stairwell.

Joe   Right.
Stairwell.
And –
He was looking out the window.
Couldn't take his eyes off the car park.
This totally empty car park.
And he said –

Emma   Go on.

Joe   He said there was a person out there.
Out in the car park.
Like a
shadow person.

Emma   A shadow?

Joe   A shadow person yeh.
That's how he described them.
A shadow person and that they'd been following him for years.
But that he could finally see them.

And I looked with him for ages and I was saying like:
Mate there's nobody there.
It's empty.
But he wasn't having it.
He said he could finally see them.
He knew they'd been there for so long and he could finally see them.

Look alright.
This was probably just because we'd been up so long.
We were –

I'll admit to as much –
Very very you know
and all of that.
Sleep deprivation.
But he was shaking.
And.

You know I think sometimes.
The thing with
supernatural shit you know.
It doesn't really matter if it's there or not.
In physical terms.
If somebody sees it
then it's real.
That's what I think.
And he saw it.
You know.
He saw this
shadow person.
And yeh it was probably
his mind playing tricks on him
whatever
whatever.
But.

I think he felt like he was being
haunted by something.
And he couldn't live with it.
Do you know what I mean?
It was hounding him.

That was about a week before he left.

Emma My God.
Left where?

Joe Dunno.
Just said he had to go.
Asked me to drive him to the station.

Emma You drove him?

Joe Yeh but.
He wouldn't say where he was going.
This was uh.
Like I said –
Bonfire Night.

We stopped on the way.
At the uh
overpass you know?
I didn't ask or anything.
I just parked up
and we watched the fireworks for a while.
Screams and bangs and what have you.
Then after a while he tells me.
He tells me he thinks he'll walk.
And he opens the boot.
Gets his stuff together.
And off he goes you know.
I haven't seen him since.

Emma Man.

Joe I think he was running from something
or someone
or thought he was
or . . .

Emma Who?

Joe I don't know.

Emma Oh my god.
Who do you think it was like.
His dad?

Joe I don't know.
I wouldn't want to speculate.

Emma Or a dealer, or . . .
Did he owe anyone any money?

Joe   Well like I say
        he lost his job.
        And his lifestyle –
        Well he didn't slow down put it that way.

Emma   That's so fucked up.
        You didn't tell me that before.

Joe   I know but.
        Like I say he'd been off the rails for a while so.
        Probably imagined it.
        Who knows.

Emma   I didn't even know he was.
        I mean I knew he smoked a bit.
        Bit of a drinker.
        Like we all were right.

Joe   Nah come on.
        He was always
        heavier into it than we were.

        Do you not remember his trick with the apple?

Emma   No.
        What was that?

Joe   You core an apple.
        And you roll a joint.
        And then you –
        Well you turn the apple into a bong.
        I'm calling it a trick but it wasn't really.

        Anyway.

Emma   Jesus.
        I'm sorry.
        That's rough.

Joe   It's cool.
        Yeh.
        Thank you though.

        ,

Emma Am I difficult to be around?

Joe What?

Emma You said he was difficult to be around.
Am I difficult to be around?

Joe No.
No you're great to be around.

Emma Are you glad I'm back?

Joe Yeh.
I am yeh.

Emma You're handsome now.

Joe Really?

Emma Yeh you got handsome.

Joe Cool.
What like
different?
Like my face has changed?

Emma Can I ask you something?

Joe What?

Emma Do you have sex with people
at all?

Joe Uhm.

Emma Cos obviously /
you're living at home.

Joe I'd say
yep.
Well yeh I can.
That's not something that's
off limits.

Emma Who is the last person
You had sex with?

Joe	Uhmmm.
	Hah.
	Yeh not really.
	Anyone in a while.
Emma	Hm.
	What is
	the most
	disgusting thing you've ever done in this car.
Joe	Nothing why?
Emma	Whoa defensive.
Joe	No I just.
	I don't know.
Emma	Well let's start small.
	Have you ever burped?
Joe	Well yeh.
Emma	Okay.
	Have you ever uh . . .
	broken wind.
Joe	Broken wind?
	Uh.
	Hah.
	Yes.
Emma	Okay.
	Did you open a window?
Joe	I can't remember.
	Maybe not.
Emma	Nice.
	Have you ever been sick?
Joe	No.
Emma	Have you ever masturbated?

Joe   I knew –
       No!

Emma   Definitely?

Joe   Definitely.
       Haven't.

Emma   Have you ever had sex in your car?

Joe   No.

Emma   Really?
       Never?

Joe   Never.

Emma   Have you ever . . .
       I can't think of anything else.

       *Emma is looking at Joe very intensely. She's thinking
       about him in a way she hasn't before; trying to decide
       if she thinks he's attractive, whether she wants to kiss
       him. Joe notices and looks into her eyes. This
       continues for a second or two longer than they're
       expecting and becomes very intense. She breaks away.*

       Shit.

Joe   That's alright.
       I'm actually.

Emma   Would that be weird?
       To have
       thought of you like that?

Joe   No not at all.

Emma   Okay.
       Do you want to try and.

       *She kisses him. It doesn't really work. But Emma
       seems keen to persevere. She fidgets with sudden
       desire.*

Okay.
Do you want to –
Um.

Joe   Yeh I dunno if we can.

Emma   I'd say come in but obviously.
        Mum and Dad are.
        Um –

Joe   Yeh don't worry.
        We don't have to.

Emma   Could we go to yours?

Joe   Yeh.
        No.
        Not really.

Emma   Ugh.
        What is life?
        You know what I mean?
        I just want to . . .

Joe   Yeh you know
        We don't have to like . . .

Emma   I know but come on.
        You want to right?

Joe   Yeh totally.
        I guess I just mean.
        You know.

Emma   We should –
        We could –
        Or is that.
        Would it be grim to do it in the car?
        Like to park it somewhere. /
        Or is that . . . ?

Joe   Hah!
        Whoa.

	I mean we could I guess.
	We could.
Emma	Yeh it's grim.
Joe	A bit.
Emma	All a bit
	Friday night in the suburbs
	isn't it?
Joe	Yeh.
	And like.
	I dunno
	I smell of beef and stuff.
	I was on the carvery today.
	Plus I'd sort of imagined that
	if this happened it would be indoors somewhere.
	Or like
	on holiday or something.

,

Emma	Imagined like –
	What just now?
Joe	What?
Emma	As in you –
	Did you imagine that just now.
	Us being on /
	holiday.
Joe	No just –
Emma	You've imagined it
	before?

Joe is silent. Hot embarrassment.

Oh.

,

I'd better go in.

Joe   Maybe we could go for dinner later this week?
          I don't know.

Emma   Uh yeh.
          I'm sorry.
          I hope I haven't behaved
          in some sort of way.

Joe   No not at all.
          You haven't uh
          behaved at all.

Emma   Ugh
          I'm gonna be sick when I get in.

Joe   Oh.
          Do you want me to come in?

Emma   No that's fine.
          I just really can't be arsed.
          I wish I'd just throw up now.
          I know my dad is going to turn this into
          a talking point.
          You know.

Joe   Sure.

Emma   Okay.
          Well.
          Goodnight.

          Slow fade to black.

                              *

          Lights up gradually.
          Joe is asleep. Garbled talk radio chatters softly.
          Suddenly the sound of a hand rapping on a car
          window. Joe jolts awake.
          Blackout.

SIX

Sharp lights up.
Joe and Peter sit in the car. Peter is wearing a denim jacket
and has a folded-down pool cue in his hand. They are silent
for a while, watching the middle distance, waiting for
something. Peter sings and mumbles to himself, barely
audibly.

Peter   Thursday.

          'Thursday's child has far to go . . .
          Bonny and blithe.'

          Peter coughs. Then he sniffs. Then he sniffs again.
          Then he sniffs his hand. Then he sniffs the air more
          generally.

          It smells of perfume in here.
          You need to open some windows
          or air it somehow.

Joe   Right.

          He sniffs again.

Peter   And junk food.
          And cigarettes.
          Do you smoke in the car?

Joe   No.
          Well sometimes yeh.
          But like
          it's my car.
          You know?

Peter   I didn't question that I was just asking if you did.

          Although it is a filthy habit.

          And you certainly shouldn't smoke if there are
          children in the car.
          The second-hand smoke

turns it into a uh /
deathtrap.

Joe   Why would I have a child in the car?

Peter   Well.
You don't know.

,

What's with the perfume?

Joe   Uh.
That'll probably be my friend
Emma.
She's.
I've given her a few lifts.

Peter   Oh.
(*To himself.*) Oh ho!

,

She a new friend?

Joe   Hm?

Peter   Em . . .
Um.

Joe   Emma.

Peter   Emma.

Joe   No.

Peter   Oh.

Joe   Old friend.

Peter   Old friend.
Right.

(*Wry.*) Going steady then?

Joe   No.
What?

No.
Not that it –

Peter   Okay.

     ,

Joe   Although.
I think maybe it could be going that way actually.
So.
We'll see.
I don't know.
I don't want to talk to you about this.
This isn't really your business.

Peter   Okay.
Just taking an interest.

     ,

You're not *really* supposed to stop here
by the way.
Not before seven anyway.

Joe   And it's funny because.
I've always felt a bit like
something like this could happen.
Like it could fall into place.
With her.

Peter   Uh-huh.

Joe   Like . . .
This is stupid and
she'd probably be embarrassed if I
you know
reminded her –
But we actually had a pact when we were in school
that if we were both single by the time we were
thirty-five
then we'd get married and move to China together.
I mean we're not gonna do that obviously.

72

China or whatever.
But it makes you think.
Funny how things work out.

Peter   Hm.

Joe   But obviously like I don't wanna ruin our friendship.
And I'm a very independent person.
So.
It's tricky.

Peter   Maybe it's loading only.

Joe   What?

Peter   What?

Joe   Loading?

Peter   The space.
Parking.

Joe   I'm talking.

Peter   Alright well,
I'm listening.
What?

Joe   You asked!

Peter   About what?

Joe   The thing with Emma.

Peter   Okay and you told me.

Joe   No I'm telling you now.
I'm telling you how I feel now.

Peter   Due respect I didn't ask that.

Joe   You did!

Peter   I didn't.

Joe   What do you mean /
you literally just asked me that.

73

Peter	I didn't ask you how you were feeling,
	I asked you who she was.
	That's a request for
	top-line information.
	Not all this extra stuff.

Joe	Okay.
	I'm just saying
	if you ask somebody about something
	you have to be willing for them to answer.

| Peter | Fine. |
| | Carry on. |

| Joe | Well not now. |
| | Like I'm gonna carry on now. |

| Peter | If you've got a problem with a girl – / |
| | Well you don't want my advice on that. |

Joe	(*mutters*) Problem with a girl.
	Correct.
	I do not.

Peter	Look
	what happened
	between me and your mother
	was something
	very specific
	and regrettable.
	And.
	I am trying to get –

| Joe | Okay. |
| | Sorry whatever. |

Peter	I am trying to say that if you have a friendship
	with a woman
	then value that.
	Because young men don't always.
	I mean
	neither do old men but.

Joe   Right okay.
        Thanks.

Peter   I know –
        Christ.
        I know I humiliated myself.

Joe   You don't have to explain.

Peter   I know I did.
        And I'd like to apologise to her.
        Because she knows I didn't mean it.

Joe   Well she's just.
        I think she's just stressed at the moment with work
        you know.
        On top of everything.

Peter   If she'd just talk to me.
        I don't want to marry her.
        Do you know what I mean?
        I don't want that.
        She's my friend.
        And I want her as a friend.

Joe   Right.
        So you don't want –

Peter   No.
        No!

Joe   Why did you.
        Why did you ask her?

Peter   It's stupid.
        I was drunk!
        I wasn't planning on it.

Joe   How can you have not been planning for it?
        You had an engagement ring.

Peter   It wasn't for her.

Joe	Wait. What?
Peter	Before I regrettably / asked your mother.
Joe	Yeh . . .
Peter	There was another woman. I was intending on giving it to.
Joe	Whoa. What that night?!
Peter	Yes. I was in love. And then she went away. And that sent me into something of a downward spiral. Albeit brief. And I –
Joe	So you asked my fucken mum on the rebound did you?
Peter	Not – (*Thinks about it.*) I mean yes of sorts. If that's a useful framework.
Joe	*Wow.* And you want to dish out your your advice about what to do if you've got / trouble with a girl or . . .

Peter   Well don't you get upset about it.

Joe   I'm not upset about it.
        I just think it
        reveals a lot about you
        and this supposed fucken
        heartbreak you're going through
        that you'd try it out on your oldest friend
        because some other woman has rejected you.

Peter   It's not like that.
        I don't know why I asked your mother.

Joe   I think you should get out the car.

Peter   For god's sake.
        I'm trying here.
        I'm trying.

Joe   Trying to do what?

Peter   (*head in hands*) To get back to something!!
        But I can't reach it!!

                ,

Joe   Who was she?

Peter   What?

Joe   The other woman.

Peter   There's no point trying to explain.
        You wouldn't understand.

Joe   What would I possibly not be able to understand
        about it?

Peter   It's very.
        The whole thing is very hard to.
        All tha' matters is that she's gone.
        She was there.
        And then she was gone.

Joe   Gone?

Peter	Gone.

They sit in silence. Then they notice something in the distance.

Joe	That's your friends then?
Peter	Yup.
Joe	Well go on then.
Peter	I'm going.

,

I know you think I'm a fool.
And that you are living through something unique.
But trust me.
It's all the same thing.

Joe	I'm supposed to tell you to stop calling the house phone.

Blackout.

SEVEN

Hard dance music from inside the car. Lights up gradually. Joe is alone, lolling his head loosely in time to the beat. He rolls a cigarette and has a bottle of lager between his legs, which he negotiates up for a swig once his cig is rolled. Slow fade to blackout.

*

Lights up gradually.
The car is empty. For the first time: no radio.
Fade to black.

*

Lights up sharp.
Emma and Joe in the car. Emma is loose clothes: joggers,
hoodie. Joe is dressed the same as in the previous scene. He
looks tired.

Joe   I'm really sorry.

Emma   It's fucken
        whatever Joe.
        Do you know what I mean?

Joe   I just.

Emma   It's just really fucked up
        to say
        like *literally* say
        I will see you at eight a.m.
        the night before
        and then not show.

Joe   I know.

Emma   Like you said you didn't have work.
        You said you had nothing on.
        Blah blah.
        I can show you the text where you literally say
        I'm gonna be crashing soon.
        Will see you . . .

        Emma searches for the text on her phone.

Joe   I know.
        I know.

Emma   HERE.
        Will see you bright and early.
        Fucken bright and early.
        I mean . . .

Joe   I know.
        Okay.
        I'm sorry.

79

Evening ran away.
Simple as that.

Emma   *Simple as that.*
       What does that mean?

Joe   It means
       that I . . .

Emma   Go on.
       I would love to know what you were doing
       that was so important it was worth me missing my
       doctor's appointment
       making me choose between waiting another month
       for a scan
       or explaining everything to my parents.
       What was it?
       I am dying to know.

Joe   I just
       met up with some guys /
       and . . .

Emma   (*almost silent*) Oh my god.
       Who?

Joe   You don't know them.
       Someone called Barney who I met at
       music college.

Emma   I thought you dropped out of music college.

Joe   Yeh but like
       We stayed in touch.
       And anyway he's got.
       His dad is some rich
       engineer who has an apartment by the harbour
       and he was away so he was just like
       come round come round
       you know.
       And I was just going to go round for a beer

but then he had all these other guys round who
I didn't know.
And the thing is
they all work shifts
so they were all like *come on like /
it's the weekend.*

Emma   Just
shut up.

Joe   Sorry this is . . .
(*Pathetic-sounding.*) I guess
I care about you.
And I'm not used to it.

Emma   Oh please.
That is such bollocks.

Joe   It's *true*!

Emma   What's true?
That you've suddenly been bestowed with some
massive burden of responsibility you weren't
prepared for
because I asked you for a lift to the hospital
and you had to get out of bed before midday?
Give me a fucken break.

Joe   That's not what I mean.
Obviously.
Look I'm really sorry.
I uh –
(*Mutters.*) Fuck.

Emma   (*rage*) You're a *boy* Joe.

*On the word 'boy' Emma shoves Joe unexpectedly
hard.*

You're a little fucken
boy.
You're the one with a problem you know.

And you should know my dad thinks I have cervical
cancer now.
Which
I can't exactly blame him for
seeing as I had to practically knock down his door
with my anorak on this morning
demanding a lift.

And now he won't stop talking about it.

It's like I'm an appliance
and he can't work out why I'm not working.
He keeps staring at me from across the table.
Speculating.
It's a total erosion of boundaries
it's nuts.

Joe   Well.
        Maybe just give him a wide berth for a bit
        I dunno.

Emma   How can I?
        I can't.
        They're in every room.
        They're like gas. /
        Like –

Joe   Your parents?

Emma   Yes.
        I walk into any room and one of them will be there.
        You know?
        They're
        ghost ships.
        They drift.

Joe   They're both retired right?

Emma   Yeh I know.
        And it's their house.
        Whatever.
        I just wish.

82

I just want some space.
I mean fuck.
How much time do I spend just sitting in this car
with you?
Right?
This isn't normal.
I literally think up excuses for you to drive us
somewhere so I can get out.
That isn't normal.

Joe   Do you?

Emma   Anything.
        Anything to get out.
        It's outrageous in there.
        The things they talk about.
        They talk about their bodies to me.
        Over dinner.
        They talk about uh
        their teeth.
        Dental appointments,
        rotting gums,
        fillings.
        It just.
        It makes my skin crawl. /
        It's gross.

Joe   It's their home. /
        You can't decide what they can and can't talk about.

Emma   Why would you take their side?

Joe   I'm not taking their side
        I just don't think they're as bad as you make out. /
        It's not about sides.

Emma   How could –
        How could you possibly know how bad they are?

Joe   It just sounds like they're
        interested in you or whatever.

Like
your dad wanting to drive you somewhere
or worrying about your health
isn't a bad thing.

Emma   This isn't about that though.
This is about me trying to manage my life.
This is me trying to protect myself.
There is such a thing as
uh
bad love
or unhelpful –
Forget it.

Joe   (*mutters*) Yeh because you need protecting from your
parents.

Emma   Just because someone is acting out of love
doesn't mean their actions can't still be damaging.

Joe   They're worried about you
and if you won't tell them what's wrong
they're only going to worry more.

A long silence.

Emma   My boss didn't start ignoring me for no reason.

We slept together.
A number of times.
And *then* he started ignoring me
so.

Joe   Oh.

Emma   Yeh.

,

Joe   What so you were like
going out?

Emma   No.
No we were not.

It was a mistake.
That for some reason
I found myself making
again and again.

Joe   Why did he stop talking to you?

Emma   He was married.
Obviously.

Joe   Oh!

Emma   Yeh: *OH.*
It's all
embarrassingly generic.
But he made it feel real and

very important
at the time.

But then it had to end
he decided
so he started ignoring me.
And that's when the pain started.

I felt this pain
and straight away I told myself:
Well –
I'm pregnant!
Which is stupid cos how would I know what that
feels like?
But I convinced myself.
Pregnant.
With my fucken manager's baby.

It was so terrible.
Such an awful terrible event
I thought it *had* to be true.
This is it
I thought.
Real life has finally caught up with me.

It was that night I told you about.
When I had nobody to call?
I was lying in bed
alone in my flat
and I started writing him an email.
A long email
telling him I was expecting his baby
and that he'd ruined my life
and that he'd better tell his wife because he'd just
ruined her life as well.
And I sent it and –
Poof.
Fell asleep.
Like a light a going out.

It was the following morning I realised I'd sent the
email to the entire office.

And *that's* the story of how I lost my job.

,

Joe   And were you?

Emma   What,
pregnant?
No Joe.
Obviously not.

I know what I'm not.
I have that at least.

Slow fade to black.

EIGHT

Lights up sharp.
Joe and Peter share the car. Silence for a while.

Joe   Is this going to take long?

Peter   Just.
        Okay.

        Peter takes a folded piece of paper from his pocket
        and puts a pair of reading glasses on. He begins
        reading from pre-prepared notes, but gradually goes
        off-script.

        Now that I'm looking back and seeing it as
        something
        distant
        I can see that she appeared completely out of
        nowhere.
        But it didn't feel that way at the time.
        She sort of faded into view
        day by day.
        I can't even remember the first conversation we had.
        The first words.
        What it was we started talking about
        just that
        gradually
        you know
        we were talking.

        You should know
        I feel like a prize prat
        over all this.

Joe   Over what?

Peter   Just let me –
        Explain.
        She said her name was Melanie.
        And she was very polite.

She said she liked my pictures and –
We had a few things in common.
The garden.
This was on Facebook at first.
Then she asked if we could email.
I don't know how she found me but –
I was excited.
So I said yes, sure.
That'd be nice.
And we started to send these letters to each other.
Well emails, not letters, but you know.
They were long.
Lovely long emails.
She'd ask all these questions.
Taking a real interest.
And these were lonely fucken days and nights we're
talking about here.
So it felt good.
And it wasn't about sex before you start.
There was none of that grubby
I'll you show mine business.
No it was.
She was tasteful.
Thoughtful.
She wanted to know silly things.
The colour of my hair when I was younger.
What I ate for breakfast.
Details.
She wanted details.
And I asked for the same you know.
She had a boy
School age.
She'd send pictures of the pair of them larking around.
She said she lived local.
Further towards town than here
but near enough that I'd look for her whenever I was
out.

It got to the point we were sending emails almost every other day.
She told me she missed me.
Even though we'd never met.

The first time she asked me for something was in August.
She was about to catch a train.
She was visiting her mum and her boy wanted to watch something on her phone.
A film or whatever.
But she'd run out credit on her phone.
Internet.

Joe   Data.

Peter   Right data.
Yeh.
And –
And she wasn't going to get paid until the following week.
I mean I didn't hesitate.
Asked her how much she needed.
Sent it straight over.
Topped it up just to look generous.
That's the shameful fucken thing.
I wanted her to think I was flush.
So I stuck an extra twenty quid on for good measure.
Can you believe that?

Anyway as time went by the requests became more regular.
Little loans to last her till payday.
Birthday presents for the kid.
Vouchers for dinners out when they were strapped for cash.
A right bill you know.

Joe   Wait did you not.
I mean did you not ever speak on the phone?

Peter   She said she was shy.

Joe stifles a laugh.

Oh fuck you.
Right yeh.
Laugh.

Joe   No.
I'm sorry.

Peter   She said she was shy.
And you know what that suited me just fine.
Last thing I wanted was her to hear my stupid fucken voice.
I was already punching well above my bracket here.
I didn't know if she was blind or thought I was fifteen years younger than I was.
But the whole thing felt fragile.
Like it could crumble in my hands any second.
I didn't want to do anything that could damage it.
You know?

Joe   Yeh.
I think so.
Sorry go on.

Peter   Trouble was she had this fella.
An old boyfriend.
But a troublemaker.
She was trying to get away from him,
shake him off for good, you know.
He wanted to move them to Scotland but she was dead against it.
She said she wanted to come and live with me but.
She needed some money first.
Tie up a few loose ends.
Her half of the rent.
Some money she owed her mum.
She didn't want this bastard to have anything on her

you know.
Now of course I jumped at the opportunity to help.
It was a lot of cash but I figured if I moved a few
things around.
I could do it.
Just about.
And I did.
Nigh on ten grand.
I asked her where she wanted it transferring but she
told me that wouldn't work.
You see he had control of her bank accounts.
If he saw the money drop in he'd know something
was up so –
It had to be cash.
She asked me to put it in a sealed container and leave
it somewhere safe.
She'd collect it.
Pay her dues.
And then she'd break it off with him and come and
live with me.

I asked her
you know
why couldn't I hand it to her . . .

Joe   In person . . .

Peter   In person right.
She could come to mine.
Or we could meet somewhere public.
It'd be safe.
But he had her spooked.
She said he was dangerous.
Following her.
She didn't want me to get hurt.
So fine.
I withdrew the cash, tied little rubber bands around
the notes
and stashed them in this old red biscuit tin.

Joe	A what?
Peter	Biscuit tin.
Joe	Huh.
Peter	Selection type box of some sort. Stupid but it was all I could find that could fit it all in.
Joe	So –
Peter	What?
Joe	Nothing. Sorry. Go on.
Peter	Well I don't own a briefcase and it seemed a bit over the top buying one so – I put the money in a locker in town – Luggage storage. Near the train station. Text her to tell her where it was. And then I walked across the street to this little café with great big windows. Ordered a coffee and sat and watched. I watched that locker all day. No sign of her. Four days I waited in that café watching that locker. Four days she didn't show. I thought something must have happened to her you know. This fella of hers he must have done something awful. Taken her away. Or worse?! You know. Because you read about it. Men just –

And she wasn't replying to my emails.
I couldn't understand it.

On the fourth night she came to me in a dream.
She cycled up to the café
and told me everything would be okay.
That she was coming tomorrow.
And that we were going to be together.
I thought this was a
sign, a
premonition you know.

When I woke up I took my mother's engagement
ring from a shoebox in my wardrobe.
Put it in my coat pocket.
Christ.

The fifth day I remember especially clearly because it
was Halloween.
Town was wet and busy.
The air was cold and
smelt of smoke.
You know?
I could barely see the locker for all the people.
It was getting late.
The place would be shutting soon.

And that's when I saw her.

Your mum.
She was out doing her shopping.
Walked past me sat in this café.
Asked me what the hell I was doing drinking coffee
at this time
in the evening on my own.
I was gibbering.
Barely any sleep.
She had to practically walk me to her car.
She took me back to your place.
Sat me down and . . .

Well it all came out from there.
As I'm sure you can imagine.
I just let rip.
Told her everything.

Your mum explained that what had happened
was . . .
What'd happened . . .
That this woman
she wasn't real.
Or that if she was she was after my cash
rather than looking for a long-term relationship.

God she was so generous.
No judgement.
Barely batted an eyelid.
Fed me.
Watered me.
Good woman.
You were there that afternoon.

Joe   Yeh.
         I remember.

Peter   I took a shower at yours.
         Felt better after that.
         I told your mum I was popping back into town to
         collect the money.
         Save myself from complete disaster you know.
         Alright she said.
         Well come and join us in the pub later yeh.
         We're doing karaoke.
         Yeh yeh yeh.

         Of course it was fucken gone when I got there.
         All of it.
         Whoever she
         it
         was
         must have taken it in that hour I was at yours.

The whole
biscuit tin.

By the time I got to you in the pub I was
on another planet.

I was so twisted up inside.
All that money.
That future I'd let myself believe in
disappeared.
And in its absence
the past
came rushing in.
Choking me.
All I could think about was your mum
and what a good friend she'd been over the years.

*Peter folds his glasses and puts them away. They sit
with his story.*

Joe   That's.

Peter   Yup.

Slow fade to black.

NINE

Lights up, sharp.
*Joe and Emma in the car. Emma wears a tightly buttoned
coat. She isn't planning on staying long.*

,

Joe   Were you in Miss Lambert's class?

Emma   No.

Joe   Uh
        are you sure?
        I swear you were.

Emma   Wait who was Miss Lambert?

Joe	English.
	She replaced Miss Shelley when she left.
	Her husband was Australian.
Emma	Wow you have
	a very good memory for this.
Joe	She retired anyway.
	Was what I was going to say.
Emma	How do you know that?
Joe	They had a drinks thing at school.
Emma	What and you went?
Joe	No.
	I was invited but I didn't go.
Emma	How did you get invited?
Joe	I'm on a newsletter thing.
Emma	What?
Joe	I get a newsletter.
Emma	What about school?
Joe	Yeh.
Emma	Really?
Joe	Yeh.
	An email newsletter.
Emma	Huh.
	Seems like a very
	old person thing to do.
Joe	What do you mean?
Emma	I don't know just.
	A newsletter about your old school.
	That doesn't seem like the sort of thing a person in
	their twenties does.

Joe   It's not a big thing.
        I just signed up.
        You could sign up.

Emma   No you're good.

        '

        Listen I uh.
        I wanted to say I.
        I came to say.
        I went to Polko's house last night.

Joe   What.
        Why did you do that?

Emma   Because . . .
        I couldn't get him out of my head.
        Since you told me about him losing it or whatever.
        I've been worried.

Joe   What uh.
        Well.
        Was anyone there?

Emma   His dad was yeh.

Joe   Right.

Emma   And apparently Polko's
        absolutely fine.
        He lives near his brother in Dumfries.
        Has been since just before Christmas.
        Works on a farm or something.
        Got himself a little flat.
        He was saving up.

Joe   Right.

Emma   He's doing well!

        He gave me a phone number.

She pulls a bit of paper out of her pocket. She half offers it to Joe who makes no effort to take it. She puts it back in her pocket.

I felt like an idiot to be honest.
Sitting there demanding answers from the poor guy.

Listen you don't have to tell me what happened.
But if something did –
Between the pair of you then.
I just think you should call him.

Joe   (*uninterested*) Right yeh thanks I'll uh.
I'll give that some thought.

Emma   I just thought you'd want to know that
whatever he thought he was running from . . .
He's safe basically
you know?

Joe   Yeh great.
That's great.

Emma   You shouldn't feel bad that he wouldn't talk to you.
It sounds like he was going through something.
I think everyone's under a bit of a cloud at the moment.

Joe   Right yeh.
People love to say that.

Emma   What?

Joe   *Everyone's just under it at the moment.*
Like it's going to change.

Emma   Joe do you think um.
Maybe you'd be happier if you had some objectives for your life?

Like where it's *going*?

Joe   Why do people talk about themselves like that?

Emma Like what?

Joe Like
they're
projects . . .

Emma So you're saying you don't want anything to happen? /
At all.

Joe No actually.
I don't no.
And you know what?
I actually can't wait until I get past the point where
people
stop asking me what I'm gonna do
and just accept that my life
is what it is
and it isn't some
thing that hasn't happened yet.

'

Emma Okay well I'd better go.
I have to uh.
I have to finish some
applications and –

Joe Hey we should go for that dinner.

Emma What dinner?

Joe You know we said.
The other night.
We'd go for dinner.

Emma Oh right
yeh.
Did we?
Okay well yeh.
Maybe.
I'm pretty broke.

Joe	It's cool I can pay.
	,
	Oh what did the uh
	doctor say?
	About your pain?

Joe   It's cool I can pay.

        ,

        Oh what did the uh
        doctor say?
        About your pain?

Emma   Oh.
        Inconclusive.
        It's okay.
        It's not so bad at the moment.
        I'd sort of forgotten about it until I got the letter.

Joe   What did the letter say?

Emma   Nothing really.
        'No action required'.
        Whatever that means.

Joe   Well maybe you should call them.
        See if they've got any more information you know?
        I could go with you if you wanted to go in –

Emma   Joe it's um.
        It's fine.
        Let's not fuss yeh?

Joe   Alright well.
        Let me know.
        Do you want picking up tomorrow or anything?

Emma   I uh.
        I don't know.
        I feel like I have a pretty bad headache starting.
        Like back here you know.
        Around here at the back.

Joe   Oh okay.

Emma   Always something!
        Hah.
        So yeh.
        I'll text you.

Joe   That's cool.

Emma   Just um.
          Take it easy.

          Emma lightly touches Joe's face.

Joe   (*raised eyebrow*) Okay.

Emma   I'll see you Joe.
          I'll uh –

          I'll see you around.

          Blackout.

TEN

Lights up gradually.
Joe sits alone in the car holding an apple.
The apple glows, yellow, from the inside, like a lantern.
Smoke gently billows from the top.
Slow fade to black.

*

Lights up.
Joe and Peter in the front seats. Peter is wearing a smart shirt.

Peter   That was a Methodist church before.

Joe   Oh yeh?

Peter   Yeh.
          Flats now.

Joe   Yeh.

Peter   Yup.

          In actual fact
          a lot of the area round here has only really been
          liveable in for the past hundred
          hundred-fifty

years.
Maybe longer.
Under where we are now is marshland.
Swamp.
There's quite a lot of it
is actually
prehistoric
in nature.
So uh . . .

I don't know if you spoke to her or what but.
I'm grateful.

Joe   That's alright.
          Really.

          ,

Peter   And what about your young lady?
          Will she be joining us?

Joe   Uhm.
          She got a job actually.
          Somewhere.
          She was only ever here for a short-term thing anyway
          so.

Peter   Oh okay.
          Well that's good.
          Good to be working.

Joe   Yeh.
          She'll be back at Christmas and stuff so.
          I'll see her then.

Peter   And you and her . . .

Joe   Yeh no that was just.
          We decided it was
          probably for the best to not.

Peter   Righto.
          Well what about your friend Paul?

Joe	Paul?
Peter	I'm sure his name was Paul.
Joe	Oh Polko?
Peter	Right yeh.
Joe	Nah he's not around.
Peter	Well maybe you should invite him over?
Joe	No as in he uh.
	(*Very matter-of-fact.*) He moved away because of me. He thinks I have a substance problem. And he said that he couldn't live while I was in his life. So he went to live on a farm.
Peter	Oh.
Joe	Yeh. He said I was a like bad influence. A shadow person. Is actually how he phrased it.
	,
Peter	Do you? Have a –?
Joe	I – I actually don't know.
Peter	Well. That's a serious . . . You know. Maybe it's something to give some thought.
Joe	I don't feel like I do. I feel like I'm just getting on with it you know.

Getting through the week.
I don't give myself a hard enough time
maybe?

Peter Well
that's . . .

Joe I think I maybe have a people problem.
They just.
If they spend too much time with me.
I make them hate themselves.
Like they see something reflected in me
that they don't like.
So they have to get away.
They have to escape.
And that's what he did.
That's why –
And it's all my fault.
I'm sorry /
Pete
I'm –

Peter Hey.
Whoa.
None of that.
That's not true.
I think you're.
Well you probably don't want to hear this from me –
But I like you.
I think you're a super young chap.

And you know the other stuff.
Drugs.
If that's.
We can.

Joe Right.

Peter Help.

Joe Yeh.

Peter   Yeh?

Joe   Maybe.
        Yeh.

Peter   Okay.
        Alright.

        You know when I was a boy I used to love to spend
        time alone.
        Doing nothing.
        Just being in the world.
        Letting it pass.
        It was good.
        But now . . .
        You can't do it in the same way.
        Time demands more
        the faster it passes.
        It uhm . . .

        ,

        What is that?
        Polko.
        Why did you call him that?

Joe   Uhm.
        Paul Collymore.
        Became Paul-co.
        Became . . .

Peter   Right.

        ,

        Okay.
        Shall we?
        I've been assured we're having lamb.

Joe   I'll catch you up.

Peter   Okay.
        Well.
        I'll tell you mother you're coming in?

Joe   Yep.
Right there.

Peter exits the car. On his own again, Joe struggles to pull himself back from tears. He puts the radio on, the same otherworldly ambience fills the car. Slow fade to black.

*

This next sequence should feel like a fantasy, or a memory.
The music continues but is joined by fireworks.
The lights gradually rise again.
Joe sits next to Polko. The light of a distant fireworks display flashes through the windscreen, lighting the pair up periodically. They both stare straight ahead.
Polko has a round, red biscuit tin on his lap.
Slow fade to darkness.
End of play.